AF225869

SONDER

Printed in the United States of America.

ISBN: 978-1-956076-03-5

PROOFREADING and CREATIVE DIRECTION by NaBeela Washington
COVER ART and ISSUE DESIGN by Royce Hegarty
GUEST EDITING by Kyra Jee

Royce Hegarty is a digital illustrator who explores genres of fantasy, sci-fi and horror with a candy-colored palette, high contrast, and tight linework.

Kyra Jee is a Chinese American-identifying writer and editor. Jee has previously supported Calliope Art & Literary Magazine, and brings years of workshop experience to *Lucky Jefferson*.

Publication of *Lucky Jefferson* is made possible through community support.

Donate or submit to *Lucky Jefferson* on our website: luckyjefferson.com.

FOREWORD

In a time when our world seeks to rebuild after being throttled by a global pandemic, *Sonder* is a part of *Lucky Jefferson*'s efforts to bring writers together and generate admiration for the communities around us.

"Everyone is their own protagonist. Poetry is the transitory permeability between writing to understand yourself and to understand everyone else. Seek connections between yourself and your strangers. Write about them," shares Kyra Jee, Guest Editor for *Sonder*.

When we pause to admire the experiences behind the veil of our friends and lovers, neighbors, and strangers, then, and only then, can we embrace the full fabric of secret moments that shape life itself. I can't imagine an existence lacking reverence to these fleeting glimpses—glimpses that deepen our own perspectives and principles.

In the Dictionary of Obscure Sorrows, the word "sonder" means acknowledging that other people are "living a life as vivid and complex as your own." We hope to encourage others to write about (or with) the idea that your life is unique to you, just like someone else's is special to themselves.

You're invited to continue this practice after you finish the issue.

NABEELA WASHINGTON
EDITOR IN CHIEF

EXPERIENCES BY

Eggs cracked when I bumped the woman
in the parking lot of Giant Foods. I offered
to replace them, but she, toddler in tow,
merely shook her head and hurried away.
Castigating myself for my clumsiness,
I constructed narratives where the want
of an egg led to deprivation or disaster,
a butterfly effect of ruin: an unbaked
celebratory cake causing hurt feelings
and disrupted friendships, a breakfast
skipped and poor choices made in hunger.
Perhaps her toddler was a picky eater,
threw a tantrum, and made her too late
for a crucial appointment. I could go on.
All day I nibbled at my fantasies. Echoes
even at night in my dreams. Cracked eggs
became a metaphor for everything fractured:
old promises tangled with other sins
of omission—so much guilt and contrition.
I envied the Japanese kintsugi, the art
of mending broken pottery with lacquer
and gold, imperfections elevated to beauty.
If I felt as if I too had splatted on the pavement,
how did the woman feel? What was she
rushing towards? Did her toddler sleep
with a night light and a stuffed teddy bear?
Meanwhile, I met others. I was overwhelmed,
almost paralyzed, oppressed by a cacophony
of lives with their imperatives and desires.
I envied the desert monks their holy solitude,
sunrise gleaming on the shifting sand, silence
unbroken except by wind or occasional demon.
Was this my demon, to shatter under the weight
of my overactive imaginings? To drown in a wave
of wonder about things I sense but cannot know?
So that was my day. Tell me about yours.

SONDER

J. M. R. HARRISON

THIS HEAVENLY PLACE
SUSANNA LANG

*In the Republic of Georgia, one plutocrat named Bidzina
Ivanishvili moved 200 old-growth trees to create the
Shekvetili Dendrological Park, which opened to the
public in 2020.*

    1. On the Black Sea

A tree tall as a church spire
bobs on the waves

and still more trees
strapped upright with their rootballs

onto more barges

    2. Valentina

*I'm not leaving this place.
My parents came here from Ukraine in the thirties.
They planted the gingko, the sequoia.*

*Now I cook dinner for those who take away trees,
whose machines gouge the soil, uproot
what's lived here nearly a hundred years.*

*That sequoia saved my life, it caught
the ball lightning that would have struck me.
I used to press against the bark to feel its pulse.*

*Those who came for the trees
are well-fed and satisfied.
They left us with empty land, but a view of the sea.*

3. How to transport trees

They widened a river
as if its course

were a thing made by men
something like a road

they could make in their image

4. Valentina, again

Now my trees stand in that man's park, the one who bought them.
Ropes hold them in place.
We did not need ropes when the trees lived here.

No one should think I will sell my place, this heavenly place.
I have two gingko seedlings left though no young sequoias.
My grandchildren will see the gingkoes grow tall.

FISHERMAN
JAMES B. NICOLA

Today he caught a baby shark.

He offers me a cigarette, as I jog around and around the pier, for the friendliness and the chuckle; I've told him almost daily for seven years or so that I don't smoke. We laugh, chuck fists.

I've seen him catch a couple halibut, the flatfish with both eyes on the same side; a ray or two, flatfish with eyes in front, on top, whatever you want to call it; some crabs, although the specialized crabbers down the pier have more luck with their baskets expressly designed for catching crab; dozens of eels; and hundreds of other fish. Blood from the hook and slime from the scales stain the wooden pier for a day or two, sometimes a week; I can tell as I slip in the slime underfoot, which is practically invisible.

He takes them home. I guess to eat. I guess it's one way to eat. If they're for a restaurant, a Chinese restaurant, I hope he knows there have been mercury warnings posted here in the past. And it's the Hudson river. Who knows what's in the water? Ditto if they're for his family.

When I was a kid I used to go fishing before school. Fourth grade and fifth. A freshwater lake in the middle of nowhere, albeit by railroad tracks. Bass and perch. Occasionally pickerel. Bluefish and catfish were rare. I'd keep 'em alive in a basin out back with a hose on 'em trickling all day. Then after school I'd spread out the newspaper on the picnic table. My next-door neighbor would see me and spread the word and a crowd would come. Then I'd take the fish, one after another, look 'em in the eyes and start. Always lots of blood from the knife, slime from the scales, staining our minds. The neighborhood girls would squeal, of course, but stay, and keep coming back. At age eight I was Somebody since I could scale a fish.

Today, I know of a baby who will never lord the seas. The baby I saw flapping away on the pier, on the blood, on the slime.

I wish the fisherman spoke more English, or I Chinese, so I could ask him what he did with the fish, and if he felt it was safe to eat them, if anyone ate them.

He knew the two words "baby" and "shark" today. I wonder if he knows the word "eyes." Said to be the mirror of, or window to, the soul.

The eyes of a baby dying are not easily forgotten. The eyes of a baby shark, gasping for air. The eyes of a dying baby shark, gasping for air, I fear, will never disappear.

I wonder if he saw the eyes.

I am not who I was.

Regrets? No: Light.

Yesterday
I felt
I was
the fisherman.

Today
I feel
and am
the fish.

SIROCCO SAILS
ISABELLA DE PALO GARCIA PEREZ

the sea waves hello, birds chirping coyly from topiary
perches. eternal chatter lost to the ghosts
of the nearly inhabited island.

Life cereal, a stolen ceramic bowl, and an empty
bottle of rosé. an unmade bed, an open
suitcase, high heels, and a mini fridge filled
with pilfered yogurt. socks, a passport, and someone
else's life in pieces.

riding the waves like I own the sea
is a form of freedom
reserved for the jellyfish
and the citizens of a sinking city.

I started writing the lists on a Monday:
sitting in a summer blooming garden
with strangers I didn't want to forget.

foreign coins, a card deck, and three bottles
of store-bought Bellini. two sleeping
roommates, a desk of novels, and broken-in
Converse. a dirty wine glass, wet
clothes, and hotel towels. my last
ditch effort to ditch myself.

the language is a deviation of my grandfather's
mother tongue, and tourists gawk
at steel giants towering over history, modern
machines poisoning the veins of an estuary.
my body embraces the gentle rock of vaporettos,
the croon of speed boats, and the lullaby
of heated midsummer nights.

I'm writing lists because I know I can't stay.
I know that someday soon I will leave
the bobbing islands and that one day in a nearby
future, this city will slide into the lagoon
where tides will swell to wash the republic away.

A BRIEF HISTORY OF JADE

DANI PUTNEY

I finger my earrings & think motherland
                    where is it   inside a boi-body
I shove tapers inside my fistulas   & hope & hope   I may touch
                    the Maritime Jade Road
     the salt of my mother's vessel   her prehistoric sea changes
                    all the ghost bodies
on an inherited tongue   is this loving myself   I give Ma a bell jar
full of bones   & tell her I've discovered our secrets
          if you crush an animal's skeleton & drink the dust
you'll hear the miners clink   nephrite swirls in our kidneys
                    I scratch my lower back raw
     to find a nugget   am I Asian enough am I Asian enough
                    I lick the blood off my fingertips   (eureka)
     I ask Ma for another pair of earrings   & she nods in conspiracy
          tells me she's proud   caresses the jewels along the seaways
of my ears   *imperial* I whisper   every century of dust
          remembered in holes   every rise & fall kissing
my flesh   she cups my cheek because she knows   *do you hear it*
I ask   & her eyes bloom   & I taste the salt   & she says
                         welcome

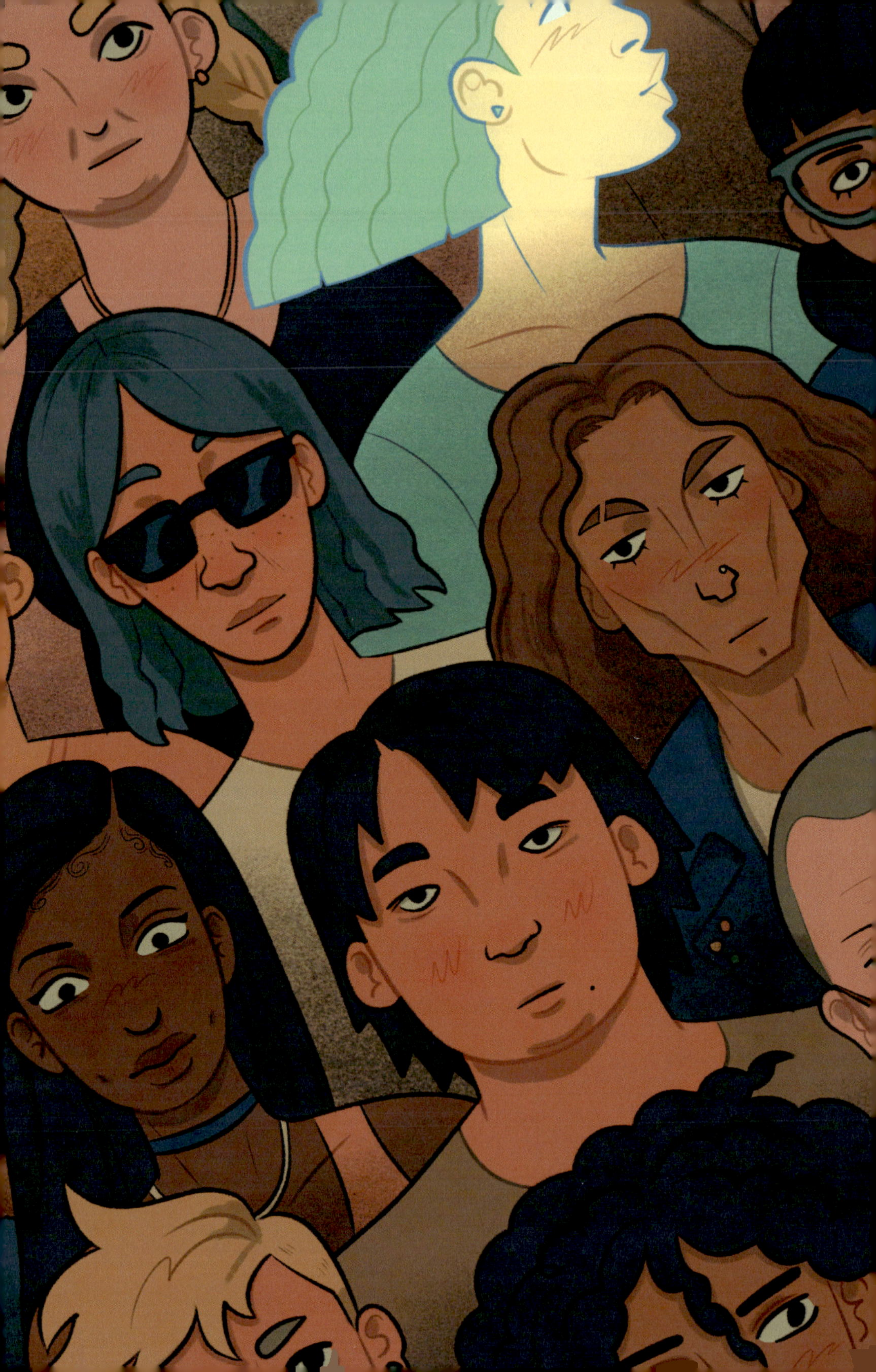

While her potato sizzles in the microwave, something on the screen catches her eye. The TV's mute button has been stuck for a week, so there is no sound. Some kind of catastrophe on the news. *Wsshhhh* in the microwave. An earthquake in China. 70,000 dead. Five million homeless. *Sizzle. Whir.* A flattened school, miles of rubble, bleeding children, bodies under sheets. *Beep. Beep.* She takes out the potato. Steam rises. Touches her face. A black-haired man hugs a black-haired woman. A black-haired ambulance driver steers his flashing vehicle from the scene, the siren filling the kitchen with its silence. Her hand goes to her breast as it does whenever she thinks of it. The pebble, floating in her flesh, rises to the surface with defiance. Cancer. She will know how bad next Tuesday. She reaches for the salt in the cupboard. Taking a knife, the one with the serrated edge, she slices the potato down the middle and pours salt into the wound.

MAY DAYS
TERRI MCCORD

"As the families of those killed in the hate-fueled shooting at a Buffalo, New York supermarket just 10 days ago continue to mourn, the U.S. witnessed another mass casualty event as 21 people – including 19 kids – were killed at an elementary school in Texas,"

— *USA Today,* May, 2022

The cow lounged
    and ate grass
languorously

while its white calf
    wobbled nearby

the chain link obscured
an artistic view

blackberry bushes prevented
getting closer

and I couldn't capture
the expression I remembered
from cows
    a pastoral trust in what
    was   about
these animals ephemeral
almost gently haunting
in the field

I put the camera down,

    purposely did not
commit this scene

to memory
    I would come back

some other place

the maydays, maydays, maydays
    and maydays.

WRITE DOWN 4 (OR MORE) WORDS FROM THIS ISSUE THAT GET YOUR BRAIN INSPIRED.

USE THIS TO START A NEW POEM OR STORY.

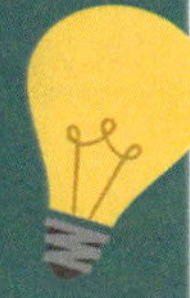

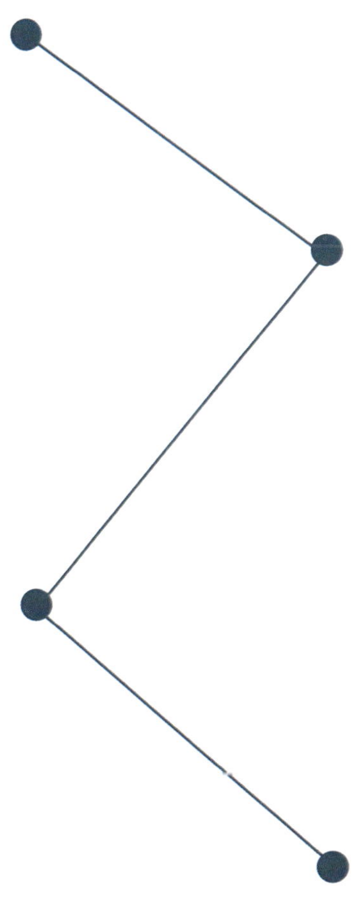

*FEELING BLOCKED? SCAFFOLDING YOUR WORK MAY HELP. SOMETIMES, OUR GREATEST IDEAS, POEMS, & STORIES, BEGIN WITH A SINGLE WORD OR PHRASE.

WHAT ARE WE SUPPOSED TO DO?
ERIC VITHALANI

The morning after Hurricane Dorian,
I woke up earlier than you.

We should have slept in separate beds.

Even for us, it got too ugly. Maybe
we should have slept in separate houses.

I didn't bother being quiet.
Half of your body exposed, half covered.

I left you that way. The dog,
spread out on the living room couch,

didn't move when I went to the slider door
and looked out. The water moved

like the universe. Debris turned
with the current, anchored into sand.

Gulls and pelicans, pigeons and terns
spread across the sky like stardust.

Hey, I yelled back at you, come here.
Look at this shit.

You always rubbed your eyes like a child
in the morning: both hands in fists,

twisting back and forth. You stood next to me
at the door, held your robe closed.

Four mile swim across that stretch of water
from Cedar Island. They came from there, I said.

What a mess. Everything is destroyed.
What are we supposed to do? you asked.

Your voice was always a little gravelly
after we had a night of drinking.

I took my phone out of my pocket, you leaned
against me. Your head against my arm.

This is 911. What's your emergency?
Hi, I said, there are three cows on the dunes

in front of our house. They seem fine, eating the grass,
but I don't think they belong here.

What should we do?

buff boy porno guru
   bending down, flashing ass
to tie the shoe
   showing tan muscle and man
if I were another I'd be -
   for fear of another word -
enamored

flint-chiseled smooth
   like foam wet
hairgel

classical
   graven
a bust of another sort

steely dan background
   rippling and tender

he speaks in dreams, he speaks in
            neon
         lowdown
            lowman
   a daring subterfuge
            the car out back

I only have to be told
   once is enough

ADOINOS (DEATH OF)

JANSON BRIGGS

homemade omen
    w/ homequeen
  brats bragging
and money, always money

we walk hand in hand thru the museum,
  me and her
and she chatters, chatters, chatters
    while I
      dream
    of being
        hewn
          in half

SOFT, DEAD LEAF
WINSLOW MACDONALD

The night that you killed yourself
I walked down to the clearing where
As boys
we had built a settlement.

As pioneers
we had cleared the trees.
And when the land gasped out
we leaned logs against boulders
and fell asleep beneath the lean-tos.

Then one night, when the fire whispered last,
the human shrieks of a dying animal awoke us.
And the next morning we found the still-steaming carcass
of a dead deer lying on purple moss
with an eye resting gently on a soft, dead leaf.
We left it there.

So the night that you called me
to tell me that you killed yourself,
I walked down through the forest to the clearing
and found two boys,
asleep under lean-tos
with a fire breathing gently
against the seething earth.

ELECTRIC RAINBOW SKY
SHEILA BLACK

(for S.T)

The person who killed
Shimi still washes her cups in the deep
sink, still spins the white
porcelain, looks for the coffee stain,
and scrubs. She still sees the horizon turn
that Kodachrome orange and purple,
those colors that seem too bright to be real.
She still practices not thinking about
the moment she looked the other way
and heard the thud against the bumper,
a sickening sound of bone crush,
then nothing. She still walks the dog.
She still kisses her children on the cheeks.
The sadness that overtakes her
more vibrant and rainbow even than the
horizon after a summer storm when
the strange irradiated sky might make you
think for a moment you could live
forever.

FUNERAL AND A PUNCTURE WOUND

TONY HUGHES

It was neither stoic nor brave holding
your tongue while the parade of homicidal cells
stomped pancreatically ever on.

pan kreas. all flesh.

I'll even take the grocery store parking lot. Around 7 when
the sun's really kissing the clouds
that's all, you'd say, always like a complaint rising up
through the mass, about the bad day you need more than I do.
I thought, *What's your fucking problem?*

and now I'm supposed to know what to do with this shit?

The stone-washed bikini?
 Your jewelry box tiered with bougainvillea powders and creams,
clip-on things, plastic brooches and tangled chains.
I'll have another Saturday flipping for triple features
'til dawn. You'll be high and I: still cranked from our midnight Frosty run.

Do you have that dirty green creek with the rope swing to give?
Catfish and snapping turtle, cleaned, salted, dredged and
fried. crispy drive thru chicken livers with one
proud
and greasy heart we fuss over like a Cracker Jack prize?

washing dishes, driving to work, walking the dogs forever
maybe the flood recedes
and the street names change,
asphalt upturned by new growth, semis stop singing,
I-75 fractured by pine and deciduous trees flashing victory leaves,
the secret meadows within you don't need you
to survive.

in my stomach something ignites and surges in strength
spreads to my windpipe
and chokes the air to live.

But at the casket the tears wouldn't come
Are you for real dead?
I pinched your nose closed,
grabbed you by the shoulders.
That was the wrong thing to do. It wasn't you

Well, shit mom came right out unrehearsed
your breath smelled like coffee and train smoke most days
so, it's better this way.
the operating surgeon seemed to think so

On state route 313 that creeps
the shitty backwaters where you practiced manufacturing me
I pump and pump the pedals of my nephew's baby blue 10 speed
 toward my sister's porch light.
atop the hill where we had been
saying goodbye, taking off ties, shedding the remnants of church.
Riding at night on a borrowed bike to escape cut rate narrators getting
sloppy on pills and past tense

behold the halogen wash and high-pitched whine of a diesel downshifting
edging me toward the shoulder so close to the deep ravine
I hold out my hand (even though I am spoken for)
having just as much a chance of pulling the sky
into the hollow below me, where I'm pitched when the truck clips my wheel.
my descent is checked by bush-hogged saplings,
one of which punctures my thigh. I could think then, barely
(I would think later-- *I was cruci-thighed!*)
lying in winter stubble
blood blossom on my jeans, I forgot, and thought for a good second before I
passed out, *Mom's gonna light my ass up for riding after dark.*

PETE'S MEDITATION

LYNN PATTISON

Time to crate the bones, then shed the bloody clothes
and close up shop. Started with fat clad lamb this morning, cracking
the knees and butterflying chops. Legs, roasts,
special orders. Hogs

in the afternoon. Drop a side of one to the slab
and you got your work cut out for you. Nothing high tech, just ax
and saw-blade, grinders. Each with our set of knives.
Got to have arms

you can count on all day: hammer, gut, skin, scrape.
Breaking bones and trimming fat. A smoke out on the dock, cup of tea
before clean up. No one left to bellyache or cuss out—
them just as sick of the daily grind.

So, of course, my noggin goes straight to the bad stuff:
card debt, the hold up with that batch of beef last week—damn waste.
The old lady's hitting the coke again, I come *that close*
to smacking her one

last night. Subtract what she spent for a hit or two,
don't much add up to pay down MasterCard. Ought to send her packing
but she's all that stands between me and the gut vat
(don't think I ain't considered it, anyway)

and most gals can't stand the stink
that follows me home. After I lock up, I'll go straight to the house
maybe coax her out to Holiday Lanes. Spring for dinner & drinks.
I used to dream I'd train dogs

or horses for the movies, leave the knives behind.
I think I'll tell her about that, and how sweaty I get when we're
Sunday shopping at the Kroger, meats tight-packed and
shrink-wrapped, dressed out with parsley in cold cases.

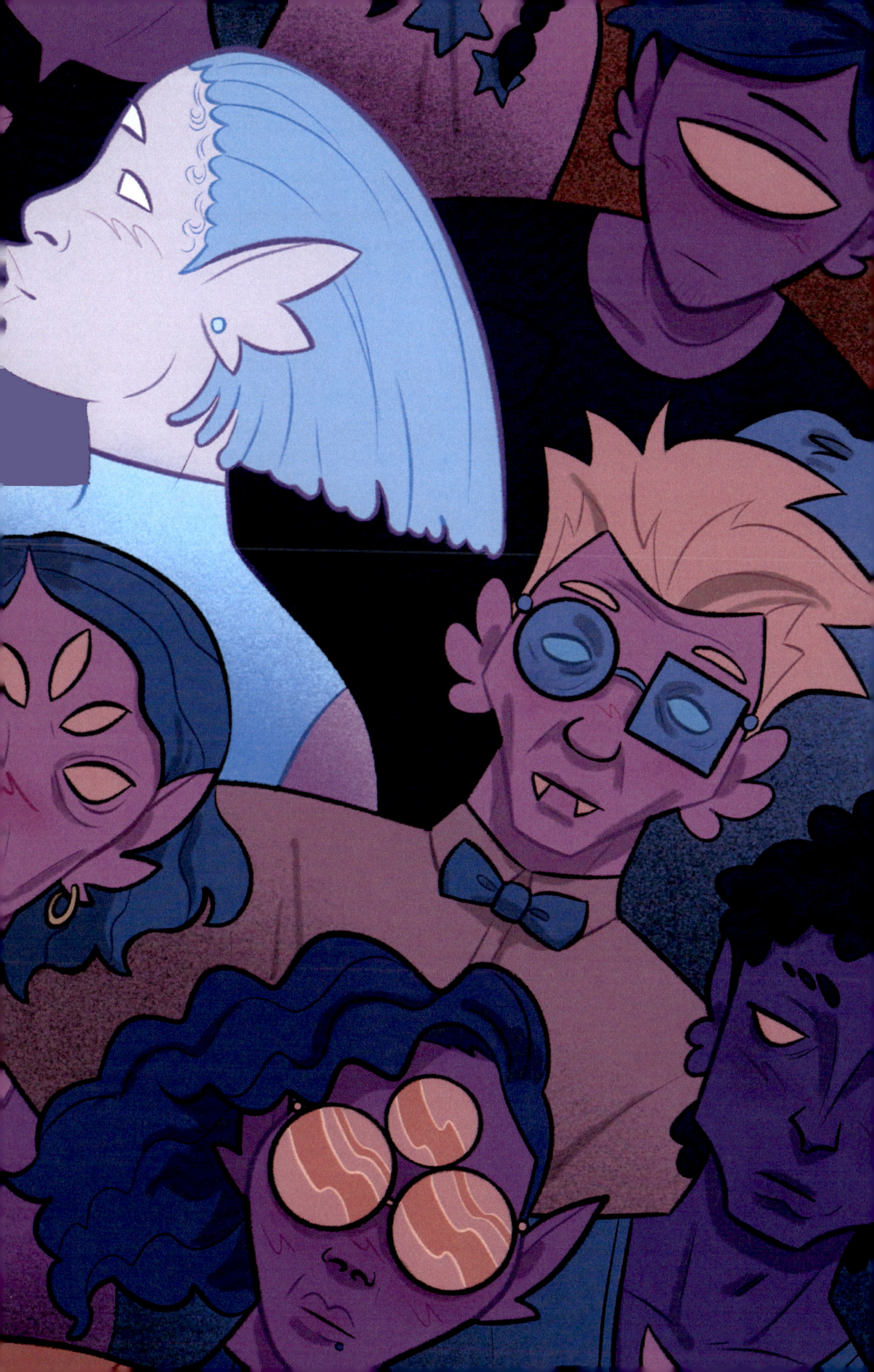

Blanched
mango veins

thread
the threadbare awning
almost wholly

white now,
a late
decayed disguise.

San Julián left
wanting
his register, rain's
renitent pilgrimage
canyons

concrete, makes
fabricating
memories of Mona's
front door

passage
impossible.

Other strangers
to sofrito and
what the store
supplied

suggest
skipping town
to a Mexican

market,
ignorant of the gulf
between them,

entrenching
the divide we say
we never notice
while working
wedges within
our valorized
stripes

to spit
out this
syzygial string
of pearls tied
too tight
about their
necks.

STEVEN O. YOUNG JR.

WOMEN'S WORK
BLKCOWRIE

"habibti?"   "yes, mama?"
"come."
she checks my hijab for glimpses
says we are to walk the streets with respect.
we are to buy groceries, not sell ourselves.
"today," she adds, "we do women's work."

at the market,
she pounds fruit for their secrets
and examines vegetables for their lies.
i am 14.   i know that what we eat
measures how we care for ourselves.
she chats with Tharwah about her business:
has it been nearly as faithful as she?
"Allah will provide as long as i'm present."
"habibti, feeding one's family
comes in many forms. sometimes shopping,
sometimes cooking, sometimes standing
in the hot sun under wood and cloth
with fruit that flirts with flies ~
here, this is women's work."
"yes, mama."
"be careful, Azhaar."
"and you, Tharwah."

we stop by Jannah's apartment
full of squalls and giggles and milk.
i sit, bored, with the entertainments
of little children.   i am 14.
"habibti, we carry children in our wombs.
even when they emerge, we tie them to us,
near our hearts, with love and cloth and
cords no longer umbilical
to protect them with our warmth."
"yes, mama. i *know*, mama."
she scalds me with her glare.
"i'm sorry, mama."

soon Jannah wishes us well
and for Allah to protect our steps
for the streets are angry and on fire.
"are you sure it's okay for us to leave
our shopping here until our return?"
"may you be as safe as it will be,
inshallah." "inshallah."

we are near, now, to Tahrir Square
the four points of freedom
where police run and threaten.
shoals of hijabs draw us near them
when mama, suddenly raising fist, yells,
"LIBERATION! ALLAHU AKBAR!"
i am 14.   she sees me shake. she sees my
saucered eyes confused by the yelling, jostled by
the anger, the echoing bullets, smoke signaling
crowd, so many people, so many more
than i knew earth could hold.

she leans in and takes my hand in hers.
"habibti, don't fear. Allah will protect us
as long as we are present for Him." "but, mama,
why are we here???! aren't the men supposed to
protect us?!" "don't you understand, habibti?
women protect the community too. men
may turn each other into candles
to burn up thoughts of freedom
but women flowered this uprising.
women made this pure, made this holy
brought spring after thirty years of winter,
for them and for us,
we must be present for its bloom."

"yes, mama. now i understand…"
i smile.
"…this, too, is women's work."

(for Asmaa Mahfouz and Israa Abdel-Fattah
along with fellow gardeners of Egypt's Arab Spring
& in solidarity with communities
everywhere seeking to flower liberation)

TRESPASSING
LEEANNA CALLON

if you could have only seen her
scaling that chain link fence
like the ladder of her
hand-me-down bunk bed

how naturally
her slender foot
slipped
into the openings
a pale eel poking out from its coral cave

landing like a kitten
on the concrete border
of the now-dark pool
dandelions and ant hills
erupting from the cracks

before I could get my bearings
she dove into the deep end
impatient for lukewarm levity

the first time I saw her with wet hair
I swallowed my gum

underneath a jawbreaker moon
we floated on our backs

the Elks Lodge pool abandoned for the night was
muted
aside from the FM static of my portable stereo
playing Pinch Me by Barenaked Ladies

she knew all of the words
and as she sang
water erupted between the two granite headstones
of her teeth

slick legs wound around waists
hers or mine
if i could bottle that smell
chlorine and watermelon Hubba Bubba
i would

whispering misanthropic dreams
into each other's
waterlogged ears
our skin absorbed the flashing blue lights
but no sound of a siren

Uncle Clipper was *simple* / the village idiot / the town drunk / gave

us kids stale sticks of spearmint gum / from his linted pockets /

got his name from the scissors he used / to clip hair in the local

barber shop / lived inside the barber shop / plastered the walls

with old pin-ups / black and white photos of Marylyn Monroe /

denying a glimpse of her panties / lined the shelves with knick

knacks / tin toys and colored glass / porcelain animals that grew

furry with dust / drank cans of Hamm's beer out of a bucket /

sank down into the yellowed tub / with Buddy the black lab /

bathed with the dog / the shoe polish he dyed his hair with /

raining down his temples /picked up the dog's shit / with his

bare hands / wore sweatpants with wing tipped shoes / wheezed

a high-pitched giggle / no matter the hardship / when the

boys from my school got haircuts from him / he'd always ask /

do you know my niece / she's a *real doll* / pull a weathered

      photo of me from his wallet / he beamed pride but I denied

he was my uncle / pretended not to know him / 'til one day

      he called me a *real bitch* / which I suppose I was / then wept

into his hands like a child / taught never to swear

SHELEEN MCELHINNEY

FOOTNOTES FROM MEMOIRS OF MINOR CHARACTERS
TONY HUGHES

[1]Benny Chaps
spooks easily.
hot air balloons,
trembling leaves,
change from light to shadow
patches of daisies and weeds--
all potential triggers
for flight.
sunlight hits linoleum fractured in Arabic glyphs
transmitting messages reserved for saviors and secret healers.
Wind driven rain
drops poly-rhythmic
plinks on his hot tin roof.
He hugs his knees and hums a tune we all hear through the walls.

[2]Hank Oats
dumps a lopsided box cake 1 piece shy,
3 candles short of her birthday age into the barrel behind the house.
Of all the green giants astride the clouds he prefers
water bugs,
minor things
piano keys in black
Trash in the barrel for burning. Half-carton
of Kools in the freezer for smoking. Corn liquor
by the quart for sleep. Drag a sleeve
over cracked lips, spit the angel's share
in the sink. He'll remember to eat
 tomorrow after another cold night
buried under blankets
where her prickly legs once governed.

[3]Nikki Lynn
Hot Cheetos & bagpipes on Copperhead Road
 make her tear up like the dust when she re-bulbs
 her mother's ridiculous chandelier.
The sadness is a permanent fixture, she yells up to Nikki on the ladder,
like it was breaking news. Aside the constant pain, sno cones keep her

summer-hands stained
 marking today as early May. nothing
but ice
and the cold blades that shave it.
Switch the tv to General Hospital before you leave, and take the rest of that banana
pudding. I'm not gonna eat it.

[4]Hazel Redwine
closes her eyes when the lights finally go down
coming attractions replace anxiety
on the flickering Cinemark screen.
She is an angular Picasso, tooth and clout of a mountain face
weapon of choice, nearly enough cash to relocate.
Their small apartment is intersecting flash points, restricted areas,
pinball bumpers that send them spiraling. Stand still,
 pretend concern
until he finds his keys.
He is all the rotten children she used to babysit.
Two consolations this week though
were meatloaf, (punching
ground beef like his brains), and half-price matinees.

[5]Cherry Chocolate
prefers silk and criminals to the inmate she married.
her stab at country music stardom, embedded in vinyl records, sold well that year.
Bespilt crystal octaves of gilded pain would blast grackles off
power lines in blind unison, but she failed to pierce the hearts
of Nashville pricks in bars,
 in boots that would never break to their tiny feet.
Yielding to shadows of marquee crooners
forever branded her a muse.
 Her trick, slipping pictures into her favorite books, worked less and less as the shelves
devolved into wall paper. Getting out of bed— like unpressing a handprint from
cement— upset
the dust gathered on her vanity.

LA IGLESIA OF THE STONE CREATURES
KATHERINE QUEVEDO

I remember how I visited la Basílica del Voto Nacional
in Quito, la iglesia of the stone creatures.

How the statues studding the outside—not quite gargoyles,
for lack of a spout—how these gorgeous grotesques
embody iguanas, tortoises, so many more creatures
that crawl, creatures that fly, creatures that swim,
an endemic menagerie of cloud-colored stone
sprouting between stained-glass arches, each front half
of each shelled or finned or feathered or scaled body ready to
plunge
          with mouth agape and splaying limbs.

How I attended a Mass there and knelt on the wooden plank.
You could see the wood's wavering, its unevenness,
its knots. How it bit my knees and cramped my legs,
but I held still.
                    How continental the distance
of the padded kneelers of my home parish.
How unfeeling.

How years before, teenaged me and my new-adult sisters
wanted to see a different church in Quito for its ornate façade,
as if entrance
mattered more
than entering.
How I asked a woman for directions to The Church
of the Society of Jesus in my best español,
how she chastised me—her nasally repetition,

"Compañía, Compañía,"
for I'd mistranslated "Society" as "Classmate."
How my embarrassment immobilized me.

How, at that Mass in la iglesia of the stone creatures,
the woman kneeling in the pew in front of me
wore a rainbow of fabric tying a baby to her.
How the infant peered so patiently around during Mass.

Our Lady of the Stone Creatures.
I remember.

Where is her child now, I wonder
with what I pray is unpadded agapē on my tongue?
Where is her child, child no more,
                                                but new-adult?

Are we not
not-stone?
Are we not
movable?

TELL ME ABOUT THE PANTHERS
JULIETTE GIVHAN

Assata,

what's the weather like in Cuba?
I imagine that it's hot, that the
heat makes you sweat, the sweat
makes you itch those thick black
braids that stick to the back of
your neck like tubers.

Are there palm trees in Cuba?
Do they have soft dark fronds
that cast shadows on your
skin, brown trunks and brown
fruit that hide white meat

that Black hands cleave with a machete?

What are the Panthers like in
Cuba? Do you see their Black
bodies as they drowse in the sun,
buy groceries in Spanish?

Do the Panthers cry in Cuba
for the things they have
lost, or in paradise have
they forgotten that here in
America

their people are still being caged?

ENNUI
FIONA PERRY

After Walter Sikert

I am thinking of   changing the wallpaper
one of us has to go   we can paste   over
the pre-exixting   layers   as is our tendency
conceal greasy smudges   mildew   fashion
        mistakes   with palm fronds

            or some such frippery

to blend   with our   other furnishings

it's difficult to remember   what attracted me to
        those flea market birds   paralysed in static
flight   their useless   comforts of   puny
hummingbird nest   carpet of desiccated
moss   laid stingily   in a glass tomb

on perpetual   Sunday afternoons   I find
myself   imagining them   laying their ghost
eggs   inside me   this ennui   is the sound
of rumbling streetcars   at closing time

            a flimsy grief

—THIS POEM ISN'T FINISHED

NICELLE DAVIS

It was a hot summer. The bank was bulldozed, because this wasn't
the sort of neighborhood that held on to assets. The month before,
I called in a dead body who'd been dumped at my door. The police
didn't think much of it, and moved it like laundry by way of
ambulance to the morgue. Too hot. Too hot to stay inside a body.

This was my art studio, illegally built on top of a garage. A bulging
second-story, pregnant with earthquake damage. I shared it with
a potter and photographer; she suffered from depression/ he lived in
New York, so the place was nearly all mine—the perfect get away
from love that had gone bad. Oranges in the sun. Too hot. Too hot

to stay sweet, even with the rind on. There were two landings, two
doors, to get in. When I went to open, the door caught on news
of a retirement home all gone under in the heat of an un-
airconditioned France; that's what the radio said on the way over.
I didn't know it then, but with the bank there came down

a colony of bees, who found their way in, but couldn't get out, of my
studio. The door stuck on their bodies, and when I bulldozed them
over with the edge of the door I could see the wood floors of the place
buzzing with a nearly dead carpet. I swept and bagged them up.
Kept one mason jar of them, because I'd never owned a jar of bees.

I threw them away with my box of used napkins. A collection of
dates and stains—all honey colored. Too hot. Too hot for my thumb
I sliced open on a piece of glass cut for a window of *Chalchiuhtlicue*—
whose name I can't pronounce. But I can tell you this goddess could
morph from a bowl of water to a man-eating frog—story of the earth

putting out the heat of humanity with her mouth. Heartbroken,
blood flooded the floor. It was so hot—the blood the night the
moment. I'm not sure *WAS*
is the right tense for any of this, though that's when it happened—*is*
happening. What is personal tragedy in light of the world on fire?

Let me tell you a story: there was a brother who, taken by the state,
was used to test Ritalin levels. His sister would visit the side effects.
Some days the brother would be trying to take his own skin off,
others he would be drooling in a corner. His sister taught me how
to solder pieces into a whole picture. We worked for Ron who had

a degree in social work, but opened a Stained Glass Shop instead.
Having something to do saves more people than social work, he told me. What
is homelessness if the State releases their Ritalin sons at 18, with no
other skills than Speed? I'm not anti anything, especially government,
but I would like something to do. It is hot, too hot to do much of

anything. I quit a degree in social work to become a poet. I'm not
convinced a poem can do anything but be a poem—though I write
as though brothers and sisters depend on it. *This one and glorious life—*
even with the jar full of bodies, light came through when I held bees
up to the sun. I cut my thumb, I passed out and came to looking up

towards heaven—and by heaven, I mean a question—one we
haven't words to ask. What invention will save us from ourselves?
Chalchiuhtlicue—put me in your mouth. I want to know home.
I've learned how pieces come together to form syntax—from this
comes context—and from this the heat of accidental prayers—

THE WOMAN WHO WASN'T THERE

SHANA ROSS

I stand in the parking lot, the sky not yet resolved into blue, the cold air chilling only the top crust of my skin, which is how you know it will warm fast, maybe even uncomfortably, as the day gets going. I take deep breaths but still leak tears, quietly enough that no one looks at me. If you grow up poor enough, you can still feel all the cuts left by paperwork over the years, like phantom limbs, aching at the first sign of additional documentation. If I tell you why I was at the DMV, you will like me less. Not because I did something terrible, but because it was a cascade of very boring fuckups I could have avoided so easily. Bureaucracy is like that, but it's a fair price for civilization most of the time. Most people don't notice we each pay different tabs.

At the precisely right time, the clumps of people around me correct into a queue, ready for the doors to open. Being early means being first to be put into another line a few moments faster, deli ticket in hand. I follow directions, one after the other. I accept side quests to gather receipts and notarized copies. Thank you, ma'am. I hope you can help me. I'm trying to… Eventually, it is two thirty, late enough to worry that I will still be in line at five, when we will all be escorted out by a guard so the stone-faced workers can go home on time.

Is it stuffy in here? Usually, I love a warm tone to my light. In this place, I feel jaundiced in the yellow glow. Plastic entombs the bulbs like amber, the lit and the dead. A darkness hums in the ceiling near where my new line is pointed. I'll be under that shadow after we clear the final curve in the stanchions.

The line has not inched forward in my active memory, which now rivals that of a goldfish. This place dulls all your senses, slows your pulse. I don't know when she arrived, but there's a woman behind me, small and thick in a grandmotherly shape, her hair piled in a nearly Edwardian updo. She holds out a Tupperware of cookies. Do I want one?

It's not a particularly personal invitation. She cheerfully and loudly offers them - chocolate chip with nuts - up and down the line. "Baby, you want a cookie? They're homemade. Smell how good. Take two. Go on." The cookies are for everyone except the clerks. The fuss is designed to make sure they know that. Marguerite has been here every day for many days, trying to get her name back.

The generous version is that she was misheard, and an honest mistake was made when she surrendered her ID last week in exchange for a new one. In this state you are not allowed to keep what's expired. "I should have looked at the card," she says. "When I took it out of her hand." She narrows her eyes and hisses a little at the woman sitting in the photo station. "I'm still kicking myself." All the shoulda-coulda-wouldas in the world, and what happened was she got all the way home and was alone at her kitchen table she discovered she had become Margaret. With no remaining proof she had ever been herself.

No passport: she never traveled. No birth certificate: she was born at home in the Blue Mountains in the 20s, written into the family bible that one of her sisters lost in a house fire in the 80s. A social security card might work, but who would give Marguerite's documents to Margaret?

I do not fact check or offer advice. I help by enjoying her cookies. Mmmmm, I say. Ohhhhh, these are a-MAZ-ing, and I look right at the clerk behind her plexiglass. Marguerite seems amused, maybe a little pleased that I am not quite as resigned as the rest of the line. I tell her about my own relatives near Asheville, and lo and behold, in this small world we do not know any of the same people. Thankfully, she does not need much encouragement to keep talking, which helps pass the time.

When I am next to be called, I ask if she thinks she will get somewhere today. She goes silent for the first time since I've known her, near an hour now. She purses her lips. She shakes her head. Nope. "But baby," she says, "I am prepared to make Margaret such a pain in the ass that someday, *someday* they will give in and put an end to that woman."

My own ordeal ended and I have since kept better tabs on at least the automotive paperwork. Last I saw her, Marguerite was in a new line, waving back as I left, the sliding doors shushing open to release me, a sound encouraging everyone who escapes to never speak of this again.

THIS HOME
GENEVIEVE KAPLAN

to enter the world
to participate in
the shopping center
weave through
the checkout line
experience shears
in the parking lot
mirrors propped
the wind
makes us peek
beneath everything
hair flying
the next
is coming
peach recall
pocket drops
underscored booklets
daring streetlights
we're invited again
plate glass and podiums
aromatics and exhaust
each gesture
unmakes us
are we
getting smarter
we read
and we lack

and we read and
we wait
we look
to each corner
the roof
the room
is overrated
we see lights
twinkle through
night sky
each window
tints foreground
brings indoors
out or outdoors
in mostly dust
or bug-shells
leftover craft
and materials
a creak inside
like a footstep
a groan
we're full
and we're filling
watching the whole
of us kink up
crouch down
and wait

SUBMIT TO
LUCKY JEFFERSON

***Lucky Jefferson*'s mission is simple:**
we publish social change.

And our vision is to see books reimagined to center the modern reader.

Founded in 2018, *Lucky Jefferson* is an award-winning nonprofit, literary journal, and publisher that reimagines books by creating interactive and collaborative community experiences that center the writer and artist and cultivate inclusion and representation in contemporary literature.

Lucky Jefferson is proud to feature poets and writers who have never been published, marginalized perspectives, and those who sought to pursue writing later in life.

Learn more + consider submitting at: **luckyjefferson.com**

FOLLOW US

 @LUCKY_JEFFERSON

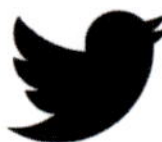 @_LUCKYJEFFERSON

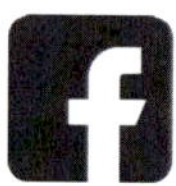 @LUCKYJEFFERSONLIT

STRIKE A POSE

TAKE A SELFIE
WITH YOUR COPY OF
SONDER AND TAG US!

HASHTAGSSSS

USE #SONDER
OR #LJSQUAD TO
FOLLOW THE CONVO